50 Cocktail Beverage Innovation Recipes for Home

By: Kelly Johnson

Table of Contents

- Martini
- Mojito
- Margarita
- Old Fashioned
- Manhattan
- Daiquiri
- Negroni
- Cosmopolitan
- Moscow Mule
- Mai Tai
- Pina Colada
- Sangria
- Whiskey Sour
- Bloody Mary
- Gimlet
- Mint Julep
- French 75
- Tom Collins
- White Russian
- Piña Colada
- Paloma
- Blue Lagoon
- Sex on the Beach
- Long Island Iced Tea
- Tequila Sunrise
- Bellini
- Irish Coffee
- Mimosa
- Espresso Martini
- Black Russian
- Amaretto Sour
- Mojito
- Caipirinha
- Dark and Stormy
- Singapore Sling

- Margarita
- Mai Tai
- Screwdriver
- Tequila Sunrise
- Bellini
- Negroni
- Gin Fizz
- Tom Collins
- French 75
- Mint Julep
- Sidecar
- Sazerac
- Cuba Libre
- Manhattan
- Bloody Mary

Martini

Ingredients:

- 2 1/2 oz gin or vodka
- 1/2 oz dry vermouth
- Ice
- Lemon twist or olives for garnish

Instructions:

1. Fill a mixing glass or cocktail shaker with ice cubes.
2. Pour the gin or vodka and dry vermouth over the ice.
3. Stir or shake well until the mixture is well chilled.
4. Strain the mixture into a chilled martini glass.
5. Garnish with a lemon twist or olives.
6. Serve and enjoy your classic Martini!

Mojito

Ingredients:

- 2 oz white rum
- 1 oz fresh lime juice
- 2 teaspoons white sugar
- 6-8 fresh mint leaves
- Club soda
- Ice cubes
- Lime wedges and mint sprigs for garnish

Instructions:

1. In a glass, muddle the mint leaves with the lime juice and sugar until the mint is slightly crushed and the sugar is dissolved.
2. Fill the glass with ice cubes.
3. Pour the white rum over the ice.
4. Top off the glass with club soda.
5. Stir gently to combine the ingredients.
6. Garnish with a lime wedge and a sprig of mint.
7. Serve and enjoy your refreshing Mojito!

Margarita

Ingredients:

- 2 oz tequila
- 1 oz triple sec or Cointreau
- 1 oz fresh lime juice
- Salt for rimming (optional)
- Ice cubes
- Lime wedge for garnish

Instructions:

1. If desired, rim the edge of a margarita glass with salt. To do this, rub a lime wedge around the rim of the glass, then dip the rim into salt.
2. Fill a shaker with ice cubes.
3. Add the tequila, triple sec (or Cointreau), and fresh lime juice to the shaker.
4. Shake well until the mixture is thoroughly chilled.
5. Strain the mixture into the prepared margarita glass filled with ice.
6. Garnish with a lime wedge.
7. Serve and enjoy your classic Margarita!

Old Fashioned

Ingredients:

- 2 oz bourbon or rye whiskey
- 1 sugar cube or 1/2 teaspoon of sugar
- 2-3 dashes Angostura bitters
- Orange twist or cherry for garnish (optional)
- Ice cubes

Instructions:

1. Place the sugar cube or sugar in an Old Fashioned glass (or rocks glass).
2. Add 2-3 dashes of Angostura bitters onto the sugar cube.
3. Muddle the sugar and bitters together until the sugar is partially dissolved.
4. Add a few ice cubes to the glass.
5. Pour the bourbon or rye whiskey over the ice.
6. Stir gently to combine.
7. If desired, garnish with an orange twist or a cherry.
8. Serve and enjoy your classic Old Fashioned!

Manhattan

Ingredients:

- 2 oz rye whiskey or bourbon
- 1 oz sweet vermouth
- 2 dashes Angostura bitters
- Maraschino cherry for garnish
- Orange twist for garnish (optional)
- Ice cubes

Instructions:

1. Fill a mixing glass or cocktail shaker with ice cubes.
2. Pour the rye whiskey or bourbon, sweet vermouth, and Angostura bitters over the ice.
3. Stir well until the mixture is well chilled.
4. Strain the mixture into a chilled cocktail glass or coupe glass.
5. Garnish with a maraschino cherry.
6. Optionally, garnish with an orange twist by expressing the oils from the twist over the drink and then placing it in the glass.
7. Serve and enjoy your classic Manhattan!

Daiquiri

Ingredients:

- 2 oz white rum
- 3/4 oz fresh lime juice
- 1/2 oz simple syrup (or to taste)
- Lime wheel or lime twist for garnish
- Ice cubes

Instructions:

1. Fill a cocktail shaker with ice cubes.
2. Add the white rum, fresh lime juice, and simple syrup to the shaker.
3. Shake well until the mixture is thoroughly chilled.
4. Strain the mixture into a chilled coupe glass or cocktail glass.
5. Garnish with a lime wheel or a lime twist.
6. Serve and enjoy your classic Daiquiri!

Negroni

Ingredients:

- 1 oz gin
- 1 oz Campari
- 1 oz sweet vermouth
- Orange twist for garnish
- Ice cubes

Instructions:

1. Fill a mixing glass or cocktail shaker with ice cubes.
2. Pour the gin, Campari, and sweet vermouth over the ice.
3. Stir well until the mixture is well chilled.
4. Strain the mixture into a rocks glass filled with ice cubes.
5. Garnish with an orange twist.
6. Serve and enjoy your classic Negroni!

Cosmopolitan

Ingredients:

- 1 1/2 oz vodka
- 1 oz cranberry juice
- 1/2 oz triple sec
- 1/2 oz fresh lime juice
- Lime twist or lime wedge for garnish
- Ice cubes

Instructions:

1. Fill a cocktail shaker with ice cubes.
2. Add vodka, cranberry juice, triple sec, and fresh lime juice to the shaker.
3. Shake well until the mixture is thoroughly chilled.
4. Strain the mixture into a chilled martini glass.
5. Garnish with a lime twist or a lime wedge.
6. Serve and enjoy your classic Cosmopolitan!

Moscow Mule

Ingredients:

- 2 oz vodka
- 1/2 oz fresh lime juice
- 4-6 oz ginger beer
- Lime wedge for garnish
- Ice cubes

Instructions:

1. Fill a copper mug or highball glass with ice cubes.
2. Pour the vodka and fresh lime juice over the ice.
3. Top off with ginger beer, leaving some room at the top of the glass.
4. Stir gently to combine.
5. Garnish with a lime wedge.
6. Serve and enjoy your classic Moscow Mule!

Mai Tai

Ingredients:

- 1 1/2 oz white rum
- 1/2 oz dark rum
- 1/2 oz orange liqueur (such as triple sec or Cointreau)
- 3/4 oz lime juice
- 1/2 oz Orgeat syrup
- 1/2 oz simple syrup
- Pineapple spear and/or maraschino cherry for garnish
- Crushed ice

Instructions:

1. Fill a cocktail shaker with crushed ice.
2. Add the white rum, dark rum, orange liqueur, lime juice, Orgeat syrup, and simple syrup to the shaker.
3. Shake well until the mixture is thoroughly chilled.
4. Strain the mixture into a rocks glass filled with crushed ice.
5. Garnish with a pineapple spear and/or maraschino cherry.
6. Serve and enjoy your classic Mai Tai!

Pina Colada

Ingredients:

- 2 oz white rum
- 3 oz pineapple juice
- 1 oz coconut cream
- Pineapple wedge and/or maraschino cherry for garnish
- Ice cubes

Instructions:

1. Fill a blender with ice cubes.
2. Add the white rum, pineapple juice, and coconut cream to the blender.
3. Blend until the mixture is smooth and creamy.
4. Pour the mixture into a chilled hurricane glass or any other glass of your choice.
5. Garnish with a pineapple wedge and/or maraschino cherry.
6. Serve and enjoy your classic Piña Colada!

Sangria

Ingredients:

- 1 bottle (750 ml) red wine (such as Rioja or Merlot)
- 1/4 cup brandy
- 2 tablespoons orange liqueur (such as triple sec)
- 1/4 cup orange juice
- 1/4 cup simple syrup (optional, adjust to taste)
- 1 orange, sliced
- 1 lemon, sliced
- 1 lime, sliced
- 1 apple, cored and sliced
- 1 cup sliced strawberries or other berries
- 2 cups club soda or lemon-lime soda
- Ice cubes

Instructions:

1. In a large pitcher, combine the red wine, brandy, orange liqueur, orange juice, and simple syrup (if using). Stir well to combine.
2. Add the sliced orange, lemon, lime, apple, and berries to the pitcher. Stir gently to mix.
3. Cover the pitcher and refrigerate for at least 2 hours, or preferably overnight, to allow the flavors to meld.
4. Before serving, add the club soda or lemon-lime soda to the pitcher and stir gently.
5. Fill glasses with ice cubes and pour the Sangria over the ice.
6. Garnish with additional fruit slices if desired.
7. Serve and enjoy your refreshing Sangria!

Whiskey Sour

Ingredients:

- 2 oz whiskey (bourbon or rye)
- 3/4 oz fresh lemon juice
- 1/2 oz simple syrup
- Lemon twist or cherry for garnish
- Ice cubes

Instructions:

1. Fill a cocktail shaker with ice cubes.
2. Add the whiskey, fresh lemon juice, and simple syrup to the shaker.
3. Shake well until the mixture is thoroughly chilled.
4. Strain the mixture into a rocks glass filled with ice cubes.
5. Garnish with a lemon twist or a cherry.
6. Serve and enjoy your classic Whiskey Sour!

Bloody Mary

Ingredients:

- 1 1/2 oz vodka
- 3 oz tomato juice
- 1/2 oz fresh lemon juice
- 1 dash Worcestershire sauce
- 2 dashes hot sauce (such as Tabasco)
- Pinch of celery salt
- Pinch of black pepper
- Celery stalk and/or lemon wedge for garnish
- Ice cubes

Instructions:

1. Fill a shaker with ice cubes.
2. Add vodka, tomato juice, fresh lemon juice, Worcestershire sauce, hot sauce, celery salt, and black pepper to the shaker.
3. Shake well until the mixture is thoroughly chilled.
4. Strain the mixture into a highball glass filled with ice cubes.
5. Garnish with a celery stalk and/or a lemon wedge.
6. Optionally, you can rim the glass with salt or a mix of salt and celery salt for extra flavor.
7. Serve and enjoy your classic Bloody Mary!

Gimlet

Ingredients:

- 2 oz gin
- 3/4 oz fresh lime juice
- 1/2 oz simple syrup
- Lime wheel or twist for garnish
- Ice cubes

Instructions:

1. Fill a shaker with ice cubes.
2. Add the gin, fresh lime juice, and simple syrup to the shaker.
3. Shake well until the mixture is thoroughly chilled.
4. Strain the mixture into a chilled martini glass or coupe glass.
5. Garnish with a lime wheel or twist.
6. Serve and enjoy your classic Gimlet!

Mint Julep

Ingredients:

- 2 oz bourbon
- 1/2 oz simple syrup
- Fresh mint leaves
- Crushed ice

Instructions:

1. In a julep cup or highball glass, lightly muddle a few fresh mint leaves with the simple syrup.
2. Fill the cup with crushed ice.
3. Pour the bourbon over the ice.
4. Stir gently to combine and chill the drink.
5. Garnish with a fresh mint sprig.
6. Optionally, you can add a straw for sipping.
7. Serve and enjoy your classic Mint Julep!

French 75

Ingredients:

- 1 1/2 oz gin
- 1/2 oz fresh lemon juice
- 1/2 oz simple syrup
- 2 oz champagne or sparkling wine
- Lemon twist for garnish

Instructions:

1. Fill a shaker with ice cubes.
2. Add the gin, fresh lemon juice, and simple syrup to the shaker.
3. Shake well until the mixture is thoroughly chilled.
4. Strain the mixture into a champagne flute.
5. Top off with champagne or sparkling wine.
6. Garnish with a lemon twist.
7. Serve and enjoy your classic French 75!

Tom Collins

Ingredients:

- 2 oz gin
- 1 oz fresh lemon juice
- 1/2 oz simple syrup
- Club soda
- Lemon wheel for garnish
- Maraschino cherry for garnish (optional)
- Ice cubes

Instructions:

1. Fill a Collins glass with ice cubes.
2. In a shaker, combine the gin, fresh lemon juice, and simple syrup.
3. Shake well until chilled.
4. Strain the mixture into the prepared Collins glass filled with ice.
5. Top off with club soda.
6. Gently stir to combine.
7. Garnish with a lemon wheel and a maraschino cherry if desired.
8. Serve and enjoy your classic Tom Collins!

White Russian

Ingredients:

- 2 oz vodka
- 1 oz coffee liqueur (such as Kahlúa)
- 1 oz heavy cream or milk
- Ice cubes

Instructions:

1. Fill an old-fashioned glass with ice cubes.
2. Pour the vodka and coffee liqueur over the ice.
3. Stir gently to combine.
4. Slowly pour the heavy cream or milk over the back of a spoon to create a layered effect.
5. Serve and enjoy your classic White Russian!

Piña Colada

Ingredients:

- 2 oz white rum
- 3 oz pineapple juice
- 1 oz coconut cream
- Pineapple wedge and/or maraschino cherry for garnish
- Crushed ice

Instructions:

1. In a blender, combine the white rum, pineapple juice, and coconut cream.
2. Add a handful of crushed ice to the blender.
3. Blend until smooth.
4. Pour the mixture into a glass.
5. Garnish with a pineapple wedge and/or maraschino cherry.
6. Serve with a straw and enjoy your classic Piña Colada!

Paloma

Ingredients:

- 2 oz tequila
- 1/2 oz fresh lime juice
- Pinch of salt (optional)
- Grapefruit soda (such as Jarritos or Squirt)
- Lime wedge for garnish
- Ice cubes

Instructions:

1. Fill a glass with ice cubes.
2. Pour the tequila and fresh lime juice over the ice.
3. Add a pinch of salt, if desired.
4. Top off with grapefruit soda, leaving some room at the top of the glass.
5. Stir gently to combine.
6. Garnish with a lime wedge.
7. Serve and enjoy your classic Paloma!

Blue Lagoon

Ingredients:

- 1 1/2 oz vodka
- 1/2 oz blue curaçao
- Lemonade
- Ice cubes
- Lemon slice or cherry for garnish

Instructions:

1. Fill a glass with ice cubes.
2. Pour the vodka and blue curaçao over the ice.
3. Top off with lemonade, leaving some room at the top of the glass.
4. Stir gently to combine.
5. Garnish with a lemon slice or cherry.
6. Serve and enjoy your classic Blue Lagoon cocktail!

Sex on the Beach

Ingredients:

- 1 1/2 oz vodka
- 1/2 oz peach schnapps
- 2 oz cranberry juice
- 2 oz orange juice
- Orange slice or cherry for garnish
- Ice cubes

Instructions:

1. Fill a shaker with ice cubes.
2. Add the vodka, peach schnapps, cranberry juice, and orange juice to the shaker.
3. Shake well until the mixture is thoroughly chilled.
4. Strain the mixture into a highball glass filled with ice cubes.
5. Garnish with an orange slice or cherry.
6. Serve and enjoy your classic Sex on the Beach cocktail!

Long Island Iced Tea

Ingredients:

- 1/2 oz vodka
- 1/2 oz rum
- 1/2 oz gin
- 1/2 oz tequila
- 1/2 oz triple sec
- 3/4 oz fresh lemon juice
- 1/2 oz simple syrup
- Cola
- Lemon wedge for garnish
- Ice cubes

Instructions:

1. Fill a cocktail shaker with ice cubes.
2. Add the vodka, rum, gin, tequila, triple sec, fresh lemon juice, and simple syrup to the shaker.
3. Shake well until the mixture is thoroughly chilled.
4. Strain the mixture into a highball glass filled with ice cubes.
5. Top off with cola, leaving some room at the top of the glass.
6. Stir gently to combine.
7. Garnish with a lemon wedge.
8. Serve and enjoy your classic Long Island Iced Tea!

Tequila Sunrise

Ingredients:

- 2 oz tequila
- 4 oz orange juice
- 1/2 oz grenadine syrup
- Orange slice and maraschino cherry for garnish
- Ice cubes

Instructions:

1. Fill a highball glass with ice cubes.
2. Pour the tequila and orange juice over the ice.
3. Stir gently to combine.
4. Slowly pour the grenadine syrup over the back of a spoon to create a gradient effect.
5. Garnish with an orange slice and maraschino cherry.
6. Serve and enjoy your classic Tequila Sunrise!

Bellini

Ingredients:

- 2 oz peach purée or peach nectar
- Prosecco or champagne
- Peach slice or raspberry for garnish (optional)
- Ice cubes

Instructions:

1. Chill a champagne flute in the refrigerator for about 10 minutes.
2. Once chilled, pour the peach purée or peach nectar into the flute.
3. Top off with chilled Prosecco or champagne, filling the glass almost to the rim.
4. Gently stir to combine, being careful not to lose the fizz.
5. Optionally, garnish with a peach slice or raspberry.
6. Serve and enjoy your classic Bellini!

Irish Coffee

Ingredients:

- 1 1/2 oz Irish whiskey
- 1 cup hot brewed coffee
- 2 teaspoons brown sugar
- Heavy cream, lightly whipped
- Ground nutmeg or cocoa powder for garnish (optional)

Instructions:

1. Preheat a glass by filling it with hot water, then emptying it.
2. Pour the hot brewed coffee into the preheated glass.
3. Add the brown sugar and stir until dissolved.
4. Add the Irish whiskey and stir to combine.
5. Gently float the lightly whipped heavy cream on top of the coffee by pouring it over the back of a spoon.
6. Optionally, sprinkle ground nutmeg or cocoa powder on top for garnish.
7. Serve immediately and enjoy your classic Irish Coffee!

Mimosa

Ingredients:

- 2 oz orange juice
- Champagne or sparkling wine
- Orange slice or strawberry for garnish (optional)

Instructions:

1. Chill a champagne flute in the refrigerator for about 10 minutes.
2. Once chilled, pour the orange juice into the flute.
3. Top off with chilled champagne or sparkling wine, filling the glass almost to the rim.
4. Gently stir to combine.
5. Optionally, garnish with an orange slice or strawberry.
6. Serve and enjoy your classic Mimosa!
7.

Espresso Martini

Ingredients:

- 1 1/2 oz vodka
- 1 oz coffee liqueur (such as Kahlúa)
- 1 oz freshly brewed espresso
- 1/2 oz simple syrup (optional)
- Coffee beans for garnish

Instructions:

1. Fill a shaker with ice cubes.
2. Add the vodka, coffee liqueur, freshly brewed espresso, and simple syrup (if using) to the shaker.
3. Shake vigorously until well chilled.
4. Strain the mixture into a chilled martini glass.
5. Garnish with a few coffee beans floating on top.
6. Serve and enjoy your classic Espresso Martini!

Ingredients:

- 1 1/2 oz vodka
- 1 oz coffee liqueur (such as Kahlúa)
- 1 oz freshly brewed espresso
- 1/2 oz simple syrup (optional)
- Coffee beans for garnish

Instructions:

1. Fill a shaker with ice cubes.
2. Add the vodka, coffee liqueur, freshly brewed espresso, and simple syrup (if using) to the shaker.
3. Shake vigorously until well chilled.
4. Strain the mixture into a chilled martini glass.

5. Garnish with a few coffee beans floating on top.
6. Serve and enjoy your classic Espresso Martini!

Black Russian

Ingredients:

- 2 oz vodka
- 1 oz coffee liqueur (such as Kahlúa)
- Ice cubes

Instructions:

1. Fill an old-fashioned glass with ice cubes.
2. Pour the vodka over the ice.
3. Float the coffee liqueur on top by pouring it over the back of a spoon.
4. Stir gently to combine.
5. Serve and enjoy your classic Black Russian!

Amaretto Sour

Ingredients:

- 2 oz amaretto liqueur
- 1 oz fresh lemon juice
- 1/2 oz simple syrup
- Lemon wedge and/or maraschino cherry for garnish
- Ice cubes

Instructions:

1. Fill a shaker with ice cubes.
2. Add the amaretto liqueur, fresh lemon juice, and simple syrup to the shaker.
3. Shake well until the mixture is thoroughly chilled.
4. Strain the mixture into a rocks glass filled with ice cubes.
5. Garnish with a lemon wedge and/or maraschino cherry.
6. Serve and enjoy your classic Amaretto Sour!

Mojito

Ingredients:

- 2 oz white rum
- 1/2 oz fresh lime juice
- 1/2 oz simple syrup
- 6 fresh mint leaves
- Club soda
- Lime wedge and mint sprig for garnish
- Ice cubes

Instructions:

1. In a glass, muddle the fresh mint leaves with the lime juice and simple syrup until the mint is slightly crushed and aromatic.
2. Fill the glass with ice cubes.
3. Pour the white rum over the ice.
4. Top off with club soda.
5. Stir gently to combine.
6. Garnish with a lime wedge and a mint sprig.
7. Serve and enjoy your classic Mojito!

Caipirinha

Ingredients:

- 2 oz cachaça
- 1/2 lime, cut into wedges
- 2 teaspoons granulated sugar
- Ice cubes

Instructions:

1. Place the lime wedges and sugar into a rocks glass.
2. Muddle the lime and sugar together to release the lime juice and dissolve the sugar.
3. Fill the glass with ice cubes.
4. Pour the cachaça over the ice.
5. Stir gently to combine.
6. Garnish with a lime wedge if desired.
7. Serve and enjoy your classic Caipirinha!

Dark and Stormy

Ingredients:

- 2 oz dark rum
- 3 oz ginger beer
- 1/2 oz fresh lime juice
- Lime wedge for garnish
- Ice cubes

Instructions:

1. Fill a glass with ice cubes.
2. Pour the dark rum over the ice.
3. Top off with ginger beer.
4. Squeeze in the fresh lime juice.
5. Stir gently to combine.
6. Garnish with a lime wedge.
7. Serve and enjoy your classic Dark and Stormy!

Singapore Sling

Ingredients:

- 1 1/2 oz gin
- 1/2 oz cherry liqueur (such as Cherry Heering)
- 1/4 oz Cointreau or triple sec
- 1/4 oz Benedictine
- 4 oz pineapple juice
- 3/4 oz fresh lime juice
- 1/4 oz grenadine
- Dash of Angostura bitters
- Club soda
- Maraschino cherry and orange slice for garnish
- Ice cubes

Instructions:

1. Fill a shaker with ice cubes.
2. Add the gin, cherry liqueur, Cointreau, Benedictine, pineapple juice, lime juice, grenadine, and a dash of Angostura bitters to the shaker.
3. Shake well until the mixture is thoroughly chilled.
4. Strain the mixture into a highball glass filled with ice cubes.
5. Top off with club soda.
6. Garnish with a maraschino cherry and an orange slice.
7. Serve and enjoy your classic Singapore Sling!

Margarita

Ingredients:

- 2 oz tequila
- 1 oz triple sec or Cointreau
- 1 oz fresh lime juice
- Salt for rimming (optional)
- Lime wedge for garnish
- Ice cubes

Instructions:

1. If desired, rim the edge of a margarita glass with salt. To do this, rub a lime wedge around the rim of the glass, then dip the rim into salt.
2. Fill a shaker with ice cubes.
3. Add the tequila, triple sec (or Cointreau), and fresh lime juice to the shaker.
4. Shake well until the mixture is thoroughly chilled.
5. Strain the mixture into the prepared margarita glass filled with ice.
6. Garnish with a lime wedge.
7. Serve and enjoy your classic Margarita!

Mai Tai

Ingredients:

- 1 1/2 oz aged rum
- 3/4 oz fresh lime juice
- 1/2 oz orange curaçao
- 1/4 oz orgeat syrup
- 1/4 oz simple syrup
- Pineapple spear and mint sprig for garnish
- Crushed ice

Instructions:

1. Fill a shaker with crushed ice.
2. Add the aged rum, fresh lime juice, orange curaçao, orgeat syrup, and simple syrup to the shaker.
3. Shake well until chilled.
4. Strain the mixture into a glass filled with crushed ice.
5. Garnish with a pineapple spear and mint sprig.
6. Serve and enjoy your classic Mai Tai!

Screwdriver

Ingredients:

- 2 oz vodka
- 4 oz orange juice
- Orange slice for garnish (optional)
- Ice cubes

Instructions:

1. Fill a highball glass with ice cubes.
2. Pour the vodka over the ice.
3. Top off with orange juice, stirring gently to combine.
4. Garnish with an orange slice if desired.
5. Serve and enjoy your classic Screwdriver!

Tequila Sunrise

Ingredients:

- 2 oz tequila
- 4 oz orange juice
- 1/2 oz grenadine
- Orange slice and maraschino cherry for garnish
- Ice cubes

Instructions:

1. Fill a highball glass with ice cubes.
2. Pour the tequila and orange juice into the glass.
3. Stir gently to combine.
4. Slowly pour the grenadine into the glass over the back of a spoon. It will sink to the bottom and create a gradient effect.
5. Garnish with an orange slice and maraschino cherry.
6. Serve and enjoy your classic Tequila Sunrise!

Bellini

Ingredients:

- 2 oz peach purée or peach nectar
- Prosecco or champagne
- Peach slice or raspberry for garnish (optional)
- Ice cubes

Instructions:

1. Chill a champagne flute in the refrigerator for about 10 minutes.
2. Once chilled, pour the peach purée or peach nectar into the flute.
3. Top off with chilled Prosecco or champagne, filling the glass almost to the rim.
4. Gently stir to combine, being careful not to lose the fizz.
5. Optionally, garnish with a peach slice or raspberry.
6. Serve and enjoy your classic Bellini!

Negroni

Ingredients:

- 1 oz gin
- 1 oz sweet vermouth
- 1 oz Campari
- Orange twist or slice for garnish
- Ice cubes

Instructions:

1. Fill a mixing glass with ice cubes.
2. Pour the gin, sweet vermouth, and Campari into the mixing glass.
3. Stir well until thoroughly chilled, about 30 seconds.
4. Strain the mixture into a rocks glass filled with ice cubes.
5. Garnish with an orange twist or slice.
6. Serve and enjoy your classic Negroni!

Gin Fizz

Ingredients:

- 2 oz gin
- 3/4 oz fresh lemon juice
- 1/2 oz simple syrup
- Club soda
- Lemon twist or cherry for garnish
- Ice cubes

Instructions:

1. Fill a shaker with ice cubes.
2. Add the gin, fresh lemon juice, and simple syrup to the shaker.
3. Shake well until thoroughly chilled.
4. Strain the mixture into a highball glass filled with ice cubes.
5. Top off with club soda.
6. Stir gently to combine.
7. Garnish with a lemon twist or cherry.
8. Serve and enjoy your classic Gin Fizz!

Tom Collins

Ingredients:

- 2 oz gin
- 1 oz fresh lemon juice
- 1/2 oz simple syrup
- Club soda
- Lemon slice and maraschino cherry for garnish
- Ice cubes

Instructions:

1. Fill a Collins glass with ice cubes.
2. In a shaker, combine the gin, fresh lemon juice, and simple syrup.
3. Shake well until chilled.
4. Strain the mixture into the prepared Collins glass over ice.
5. Top up with club soda, leaving some room at the top.
6. Stir gently to combine.
7. Garnish with a lemon slice and a maraschino cherry.
8. Serve and enjoy your classic Tom Collins!

French 75

Ingredients:

- 1 1/2 oz gin
- 3/4 oz fresh lemon juice
- 1/2 oz simple syrup
- Champagne or sparkling wine
- Lemon twist for garnish

Instructions:

1. Fill a shaker with ice cubes.
2. Add the gin, fresh lemon juice, and simple syrup to the shaker.
3. Shake well until thoroughly chilled.
4. Strain the mixture into a champagne flute.
5. Top off with champagne or sparkling wine.
6. Gently stir to combine.
7. Garnish with a lemon twist.
8. Serve and enjoy your classic French 75!

Mint Julep

Ingredients:

- 2 oz bourbon
- 1/2 oz simple syrup
- 6-8 fresh mint leaves
- Crushed ice
- Mint sprig for garnish

Instructions:

1. In a julep cup or rocks glass, muddle the mint leaves with the simple syrup to release the flavor.
2. Fill the glass with crushed ice.
3. Pour the bourbon over the ice.
4. Stir gently to mix the ingredients and chill the drink.
5. Add more crushed ice if needed to fill the glass.
6. Garnish with a mint sprig.
7. Serve and enjoy your classic Mint Julep!

Sidecar

Ingredients:

- 2 oz cognac or brandy
- 3/4 oz triple sec or Cointreau
- 3/4 oz fresh lemon juice
- Sugar for rimming (optional)
- Lemon twist for garnish

Instructions:

1. If desired, rim the edge of a cocktail glass with sugar. To do this, wet the rim with a lemon wedge, then dip it into a shallow dish of sugar.
2. Fill a shaker with ice cubes.
3. Add the cognac, triple sec (or Cointreau), and fresh lemon juice to the shaker.
4. Shake well until thoroughly chilled.
5. Strain the mixture into the prepared cocktail glass.
6. Garnish with a lemon twist.
7. Serve and enjoy your classic Sidecar!

Sazerac

Ingredients:

- 2 oz rye whiskey
- 1 sugar cube
- 3 dashes Peychaud's Bitters
- Absinthe or absinthe substitute
- Lemon peel for garnish

Instructions:

1. Rinse a chilled old-fashioned glass with absinthe or absinthe substitute, then discard the excess.
2. In a separate glass, muddle the sugar cube with Peychaud's Bitters until dissolved.
3. Add the rye whiskey to the glass with the sugar and bitters, along with ice.
4. Stir until well chilled.
5. Strain the mixture into the prepared old-fashioned glass.
6. Express the oil from a lemon peel over the drink by twisting it over the surface, then discard the peel or use it as garnish.
7. Serve and enjoy your classic Sazerac!

Cuba Libre

Ingredients:

- 2 oz light rum
- 4 oz cola
- 1/2 oz fresh lime juice
- Lime wedge for garnish
- Ice cubes

Instructions:

1. Fill a highball glass with ice cubes.
2. Pour the light rum over the ice.
3. Squeeze the fresh lime juice into the glass.
4. Top off with cola, leaving some room at the top of the glass.
5. Stir gently to combine.
6. Garnish with a lime wedge.
7. Serve and enjoy your classic Cuba Libre!

Manhattan

Ingredients:

- 2 oz rye whiskey or bourbon
- 1 oz sweet vermouth
- 2 dashes Angostura bitters
- Maraschino cherry for garnish
- Orange twist for garnish (optional)
- Ice cubes

Instructions:

1. Fill a mixing glass or cocktail shaker with ice cubes.
2. Pour the rye whiskey or bourbon, sweet vermouth, and Angostura bitters over the ice.
3. Stir well until the mixture is well chilled.
4. Strain the mixture into a chilled cocktail glass or coupe glass.
5. Garnish with a maraschino cherry.
6. Optionally, garnish with an orange twist by expressing the oils from the twist over the drink and then placing it in the glass.
7. Serve and enjoy your classic Manhattan!

Bloody Mary

Ingredients:

- 1 1/2 oz vodka
- 3 oz tomato juice
- 1/2 oz fresh lemon juice
- 1 dash Worcestershire sauce
- 2 dashes hot sauce (such as Tabasco)
- Pinch of celery salt
- Pinch of black pepper
- Celery stalk, lemon wedge, and/or olive for garnish
- Ice cubes

Instructions:

1. Fill a shaker with ice cubes.
2. Add the vodka, tomato juice, fresh lemon juice, Worcestershire sauce, hot sauce, celery salt, and black pepper to the shaker.
3. Shake well until the mixture is thoroughly chilled.
4. Strain the mixture into a highball glass filled with ice cubes.
5. Garnish with a celery stalk, lemon wedge, and/or olive.
6. Optionally, you can rim the glass with salt or a mix of salt and celery salt for extra flavor.
7. Serve and enjoy your classic Bloody Mary!